"Thy word is a lamp unto thy feet" Psalm-
119:105
I appreciate your gift-
Always, Delana 4 /4/09

LIFT EVERY VOICE

A CELEBRATION OF FREEDOM

Compiled by Dan Zadra

Designed by Kobi Yamada and Steve Potter

Fenton, Michigan

This book is dedicated to W.S.M.

ACKNOWLEDGEMENTS

The quotations in this book were gathered lovingly but unscientifically over several years and/or were contributed by many friends and clients. To the authors, contributors and original sources, our thanks, and where appropriate, our apologies. —The Editors

WITH SPECIAL THANKS TO

Jason Aldrich, Ralph Anderson, Gerry Baird, Jay Baird, Neil Beaton, Sherrill Carlson, Ray Clarke, Doug Cruikshank, Jim Darragh, Josie and Rob Estes, Dr. Marion S. Ferszt, John Edward Goll, Jennifer Hurwitz, Beth Keane, Liam Lavery, Connie McMartin, Teri O'Brien, Janet Potter & family, Burt Ribnick, Diane Roger, Bill Shaw, Cristal Spurr, Sam Sundquist, Russell W. Swank, Jenica Wilkie, the Willis family, Robert & Val Yamada, Tote Yamada, Annie Zadra, August and Arline Zadra, Fred Zadra, Gus and Rosie Zadra.

CREDITS

Compiled by Dan Zadra
Edited by W.P.M. II
Designed by Kobi Yamada and Steve Potter

ISBN: 1-888387-98-X

Printed in Hong Kong

In every community
there is work to be done.
In every nation, there
are wounds to heal.
In every heart there is
the power to do it.

—MARIANNE WILLIAMSON

MY CO

U N T R Y

We go forth

all to seek America.

And in the seeking

we create her.

—WALDO FRANK

The history of every country
begins in the heart of a man or a woman.

—WILLA CATHER

Our country is not made up of stocks
or bonds or gold—it is comprised of the
splendid thoughts in the minds and
hearts of the people who live here.

—BENJAMIN HARRISON

Territory is but the body of a nation. The people—
you and I—who inhabit its hills and valleys
are its soul, its spirit, its life.

—JAMES A. GARFIELD

We have a place, all of us, in this story;
a story we continue, but whose end we will
not see. It is the story of a new world that became
a friend and liberator of the old, the story of a
society that became a servant of freedom, the
story of a power that went into the world to protect
but not to conquer. It is the American story—
a story of flawed and fallible people, united across
the generations by grand and enduring ideals.
The grandest of these ideals is an unfolding
American principle that everyone belongs,
that everyone deserves a chance, that no
insignificant person was ever born.

—GEORGE W. BUSH

What makes America great is not
primarily its greatest people, but the
stature of its innumerable everyday ones.

—JOSE ORTEGA Y GASSET

Ordinary Americans are extraordinary.
Nowhere else on earth are people so easy with
each other, so free, and resilient. Nowhere is there
less awe of authority, less bending to tradition.
Nowhere more ingenuity and resourcefulness
and energy and laughter; nowhere more genuine
belief in men's capacity to get what they want.
Nowhere so much wealth, economic power,
technological development. Nowhere such
potential for world leadership—all emanating
from everyday citizens.

—LILLIAN SMITH

The world knows very little about its heroes. Each day unknown men and women do great deeds, speak great words and suffer noble sorrows.

—CHARLES READE

Those who say that there are no heroes just don't know where to look. You can see heroes every day going in and out of factory gates. Others, a handful in numbers, produce enough food to feed all of us and then the world beyond. You meet heroes across a counter—individuals and families whose taxes support their country and whose voluntary gifts support church, charity, culture, art, and education. Their patriotism is quiet but deep. Their values sustain our national life.

—RONALD REAGAN

Act as if what you do
makes a difference. It does.

—WILLIAM JAMES

There is one thing that America knows well,
and that she teaches as a great and precious
lesson to those who come into contact with her
amazing adventure: That is the value and
dignity of common humanity, the value
and dignity of each and every person.

—JACQUES MARITAIN

Some people strengthen our society just by
being the kind of people they are.

—JOHN W. GARDNER

One person *can* make a difference,
and every person must try.

—JOHN F. KENNEDY

Few of us will do the spectacular deeds of
heroism that spread themselves across the pages
of our newspapers in big black headlines. But we
can all be heroic in the little things of everyday life.
We can do the helpful things, say the kind words,
meet the difficulties with courage and high hearts,
stand up for the right when the cost is high,
keep our word even though it means sacrifice,
be a giver instead of a destroyer. Often this quiet,
humble heroism is the greatest heroism of all.

—WILFRED A. PETERSON

MY COUNTRY

The spirit of a nation derives
from the integrity of the home.

—MARGARET MEAD

Fathers and mothers, if you have children,
they must come first. Your success as a family,
and our success as a society, depends not on
what happens at the White House, but on
what happens at your house.

—BARBARA BUSH

The walks and talks we have with our
two-year-olds in red boots have a great deal to do
with the values they will cherish as adults.

—EDITH F. HUNTER

In love of home, the love of country has its rise.

—CHARLES DICKENS

My signature appears on $60 billion
of U.S. currency. More importantly, however,
is the signature that appears on my life—the
strong, proud, assertive handwriting of a
loving mother and father.

—KATHERINE D. ORTEGA,
FORMER U.S. TREASURER

We mothered this nation. And we have no
intention of abandoning our roles as nurturer
or wife, mother, loving daughter, tax-paying
citizen, homemaker, breadwinner.

—LIZ CARPENTER

The beauty of a democracy is
that no matter how humbly a child is born,
he has a chance to master the minds and lead
the imagination of the whole nation.

—WOODROW WILSON

My country owes me no debt. It gave me, as it
gives every boy and girl, a chance; and now I have the
honor and the obligation to do something in return.

—HERBERT HOOVER

And so, my fellow Americans, ask not what
your country can do for you. Ask what
you can do for your country.

—JOHN F. KENNEDY

Where, after all, does America
and universal human rights begin?
In small places, close to home.

—ELEANOR ROOSEVELT

We are all trying to make a big difference,
not realizing the small difference we make
for each other every day.

—DAPHNE KINGMA

Everyone has the power for greatness—
not for fame but greatness—because
greatness is determined by service.

—MARTIN LUTHER KING, JR.

You can't prove you're an American
by waving Old Glory.

—HELEN GAHAGAN DOUGLAS

What we need are critical lovers of
America—patriots who express their faith
in their country by working to improve it.

—HUBERT H. HUMPHREY

I don't know much about patriotism but I know
what I like. The U.S. Constitution. I like that. The
sight of fellow citizens doing something generous
for one another. The knowledge that we belong to
a system dedicated to equal stature. Such things
make most of us feel good about our country.

—ROGER ROSENBLATT

From a distance there is harmony and it echoes through the land. It's the voice of hope. It's the voice of peace. It's the voice of every man.

—JULIE GOLD

Our nation advances only by the extra achievements of the individual. You are the individual.

—CHARLES TOWNE

I am only one, but still I am one. I cannot do everything, but still I can do something. And because I cannot do everything, I will not refuse to do the something I can do.

—EDWARD EVERETT HALE

THEE

We are a nation of communities...

a brilliant diversity spread like

stars, like a thousand points of

light in a broad and peaceful sky.

—GEORGE BUSH

The mind supplies the idea
of a nation, but what gives the idea
its force is a community of dreams.

—ANDRE MALRAUX

Some of us have chosen America as the land
of our adoption; the rest have come from those
who did the same. For this reason we have
some right to consider ourselves a picked group,
a group of those who had the courage to break from
the past and brave the dangers and the loneliness
of a strange land. What was the object that nerved
us, or those that went before us, to this choice?
We sought liberty; freedom from oppression,
freedom from want, freedom to be ourselves.

—LEARNED HAND

Where we come from in America no longer signifies anything—it's where we go, and what we do when we get there, that tells us who we are and how we contribute.

—ANNA QUINDLEN

Each of us has a spark of life inside us, and we must set off that spark in one another.

—KENNY AUSUBEL

One cannot be an American in the best sense by going about saying that one is an American. It is necessary to feel America, like America, love America, and then work at it.

—GEORGIA O'KEEFE

The essence of the United States
is to be found, not just in its great cities,
but in its small towns. This cannot be said
of any other country. The American village is
a small edition of the whole country, in its
civil government, its press, its schools, its banks,
its town hall, its census, and its spirit.

—DOMINGO FAUSTINO SARMIENTO

Every gathering of Americans—whether
a few on the porch of a crossroads store
or massed thousands in a great stadium—
is the possessor of a potentially
immeasurable influence on the future.

—DWIGHT D. EISENHOWER

We are a nation of communities,
of tens and tens of thousands of ethnic,
religious, social, business, labor union,
neighborhood, regional and other organizations,
all of them varied, voluntary and unique.
A brilliant diversity spread like stars,
like a thousand points of light in a broad
and peaceful sky.

—GEORGE BUSH

I believe that one of the most important
things to learn in life is that you can make
a difference in your own community
no matter who you are or where you live.

—ROSALYNN CARTER

We believe we must be the family of
America, recognizing that at the heart of
the matter we are bound one to another.

—MARIO CUOMO

When the term "community" is used, the notion
that typically comes to mind is a place in which
people know and care for one another—the kind of
place in which people do not merely ask "How are
you?" as a formality, but care about the answer.

—AMITAI ETZIONI

We can do more than belong,
we can participate.

—MAYA ANGELOU

Democracy is not a spectator sport.

—MARIAN WRIGHT EDELMAN

You will find people who want to be carried
on the shoulders of others, who think that the
world owes them a living. They don't seem to see
that we must lift together and pull together.

—HENRY FORD

I'm tired of hearing it said that democracy
doesn't work. It isn't supposed to work—
we are supposed to work it.

—ALEXANDER WOOLLCOTT

It isn't enough to talk about peace
and freedom. One must believe in it.
And it isn't enough to believe in it.
One must work at it.

—ELEANOR ROOSEVELT

Excellence does not begin in Washington D.C.,
it begins in the individual heart, the home,
the neighborhood, the community.

—RONALD REAGAN

The real friend of his country is the person who
believes in excellence, seeks for it, fights for it,
defends it, and tries to produce it.

—MORLEY CALLAGHAN

Some people give time, some money,
some their skills and connections,
some literally give their life's blood...
but everyone has something to give.

—BARBARA BUSH

Each of us can look back upon someone
who made a great difference in our lives, often
a teacher whose wisdom or simple acts of caring
made an impression upon us at a formative time.
In all likelihood, it was someone who sought
no recognition, but the impact of their character
and kindness on our lives was heroic.

—STEPHEN M. WOLF

Many define America in one word,
"competition." But I have traveled
throughout this land, and I have come
away with a better word—*cooperation*.

—DWIGHT D. EISENHOWER

★

There are precious few Einsteins among us.
Most brilliance arises from ordinary people
working together in extraordinary ways.

—ROGER VON OECH

★

When different talents and ideas rub up against
each other, there is friction, yes. But also sparks,
fire, light and—eventually—brilliance!

—NANCIE O'NEILL

Whatever America hopes to
bring to pass in the world must
first come to pass in the heart of America.

—DWIGHT D. EISENHOWER

When you cease to make a contribution
you begin to die.

—ELEANOR ROOSEVELT

Few will have the greatness to bend history itself;
but each of us can work to change a small portion
of events, and in the total of all those acts will
be written the history of this generation.

—ROBERT F. KENNEDY

Our immediate future as Americans
may depend upon the living we make, but
the future of America depends upon the life
we live and the services we render.

—WILLIAM J.H. BOETCKER

★

Because their actions come from the heart,
Americans excite an admiration that must be
felt on the spot to be understood.

—JAMES BRYCE,
BRITISH HISTORIAN

★

I don't care what problems we have in this
country—they can be solved by people
coming together and organizing.

—DOLORES HUERTA

Democracy is not a tearing-down; it is a building-up. It does not destroy; it fulfills.

—CALVIN COOLIDGE

We must exchange the philosophy of excuses—what I am is beyond my control—for the philosophy of responsibility.

—BARBARA JORDAN

The future belongs to those who believe in the beauty of their dreams. In the long run, we really do shape our own lives; and then together we shape the world around us. The process never ends until we die, and the choices we make are ultimately our responsibility.

—ELEANOR ROOSEVELT

SWEET LAND

OF LIBERTY

Dreams, freedom

and dedication

are a powerful

combination

for good.

—WILLIAM LONGGOOD

The United States is the
only country with a known birthday.

—JAMES G. BLAINE

Yesterday the greatest question was
decided which ever was debated in America.
A resolution was passed without one dissenting
colony, that these United Colonies are, and of
right ought to be, free and independent States.

—JOHN ADAMS

America was established not to create wealth but
to realize a vision, to realize an ideal, to discover
and maintain liberty among men.

—WOODROW WILSON

Ours is the only country
deliberately founded on a good idea.

—JOHN GUNTHER

As America has shown us, all great things
are simple, and many can be expressed in a
single word: freedom; justice; honor; hope.

—WINSTON CHURCHILL

The idea that 280 million men and women
of different colors, nationalities and religions
could live and work productively together in
peace and freedom is nothing but a dream—
the American Dream. Hold on to it.

—GIL ATKINSON

My God! How little do my countrymen know
what precious blessings they are in possession of,
and which no other people on earth enjoy!

—THOMAS JEFFERSON

Kings we never had among us.
Nobles we never had. Nothing hereditary ever
existed in the country; nor will the country
require or admit of any such thing. But governors
and councils we have always had, as well as
representatives of the people.

—JOHN ADAMS

I know no safe depository of the ultimate powers
of society but the people themselves.

—THOMAS JEFFERSON

Why is the Constitution of the United States
so exceptional? Just three words: *We the people*.
We are a nation that has a government—
not the other way around. And that makes
us special among the nations of the earth.

—RONALD REAGAN

As citizens of this democracy, you are the
rulers and the ruled, the lawgivers and the
law-abiding, the beginning and the end.

—ADLAI E. STEVENSON

We stand for freedom. That is our conviction
for ourselves; that is our commitment to others.

—JOHN F. KENNEDY

None who have always been free can
understand the terrible fascinating power
of the hope of freedom to those who are not free.

—PEARL S. BUCK

When I found I had crossed that line (to freedom),
I looked at my hands to see if I was the same
person. There was such a glory over everything;
the sun came like gold through the trees and the
fields, and I felt like I was in heaven.

—HARRIET TUBMAN

The purpose of freedom is to
create it for others.

—BERNARD MALAMUD

Americans must not only affirm
the brotherhood of man, we must live it.

—HENRY CODMAN POTTER

America is not just a power, it is a promise.
It is not enough for our country to be
extraordinary in might; it must be exemplary
in meaning. Our honor and our role in the
world finally depend on the living proof
that we are a just society.

—NELSON ROCKEFELLER

What the people want is very simple. They want
an America as good as its promise.

—BARBARA JORDAN

We are, of course, a nation of differences.
Those differences don't make us weak.
They are the source of our strength.

—JIMMY CARTER

Remember always that you not only
have the right to be an individual,
you have an obligation to be one.

—ELEANOR ROOSEVELT

That which is to be most admired in America
is oneness and not sameness. Sameness is the
worst thing that could happen to the people of
this country. To make all people the same would
lower our country, but oneness would raise it.

—RABBI STEPHEN S. WISE

E Pluribus Unum. (One from many).

—MOTTO FOR THE UNITED STATES SEAL

Let us begin to see the true promise
of our country, not as a melting pot,
but as a kaleidoscope.

—ROBERT F. KENNEDY

Our flag is red, white and blue, but our nation is
a rainbow—red, brown, black and white—and we're
all precious in God's sight. America is not like a
blanket—one piece of unbroken cloth…America
is more like a quilt—many patches, many pieces,
many colors, many sizes, all woven and held
together by a common thread.

—JESSE JACKSON

We hold these truths to be self-evident,
that all men—and women—are created equal.

—ELIZABETH CADY STANTON

Instead of this absurd division
into sexes they ought to class people
as static or dynamic.

—EVELYN WAUGH

If there must be a stereotype, let it have nothing
to do with race, creed, color, gender or advantage.
Let it have everything to do with effort, energy,
ideas, commitment and capabilities.

—DAN ZADRA

Accomplishments have no color.

—LEONTYNE PRICE

Do not call for black power or green power.
Call for brain power.

—BARBARA JORDAN

If you want to see real brotherhood in action,
just watch American high school kids taking
a final exam. There's no question of race,
creed, or color. There is only one question:
"Who's got the answer?"

—SAM LEVENSON

Those who expect to reap the
blessings of freedom must undergo
the fatigue of supporting it.

—THOMAS PAINE

Liberty comes with responsibility.
Voting is a civic sacrament.

—THEODORE M. HESBURGH

Our Constitution and Bill of Rights are the
envy of the entire world, and yet how many
Americans can actually recite them?

—ELIZABETH DOLE

I've read your Bill of Rights a hundred times and I'll probably read it a hundred more before I die. I'm not sure the American people have any idea how blessed they are to have the Bill of Rights. After all, who needs a document to guarantee rights that people already presume they have? Ask the people who tore down fences and jumped walls. Ask the people who were cutoff from their families and deprived of their jobs. Ask my fellow workers at the Gdansk shipyard. Freedom may be the soul of humanity, but sometimes you have to struggle to prove it.

—LECH WALESA,
POLISH NOBEL PEACE LAUREATE

If our democracy is to flourish,
it must have criticism; if our government
is to function, it must have dissent.

—HENRY STEELE COMMAGER

Let no one think for a moment, however,
that national debate means national division.

—LYNDON B. JOHNSON

There is no "Republican," no "Democrat,"
on the Fourth of July—all are Americans,
and their country is greater than party.

—JAMES G. BLAINE

In the end, Liberty is a pattern of life
shared by free people: The right to go to
a church with a cross, star, dome or steeple;
the right to shout your opinions 'til your
tonsils are worn to a frazzle; the right to go to
school, to enter a profession, to earn an honest
living; and the obligation to do an honest day's
work; the right to put your side of the argument
in the hands of a jury. The right to choose who
shall run our government, and the obligation
to guard that right and keep it clean.
The right to hope, dream and pray—
and the obligation to serve.

—HAL BORLAND

OF THE

I SING

America is a tune.

It must be sung

together.

—GERALD STANLEY LEE

Sometimes people call me an idealist.
Well, that is the way I know I am an American.
America is the only idealist nation in the world.

—WOODROW WILSON

It is a fabulous country, it is the
only place where miracles not only happen,
but where they happen all the time.

—THOMAS WOLFE

This is a wonderful country. This is a great place.
Sometimes we don't see it. But I encourage people
to look a little bit harder because if you look with
your heart, if you look with hope, you will find a
people and a country and a world worth living in.

—RON KOVIK

It is a noble land that God has given us;
a land that can feed and clothe the world;
a land whose coastlines would enclose half the
countries of Europe; a land set like a sentinel
between the two imperial oceans of the globe.

—ALBERT J. BEVERIDGE

But America's most priceless asset is not
its natural resources, or its matchless wealth,
or its unprecedented power. It is the character
of its people, their indomitable self-confidence,
their sleepless initiative and, above all,
their irrepressible optimism.

—B.C. FORBES

The map of America is a map of
endlessness, of opening out, of forever and ever.
No American's face would make you think of it
but his hope might, his courage might.

—ARCHIBALD MACLEISH

The happy ending is our national belief.

—MARY MCCARTHY

America grew great from the seed of the will
to do and dare; the will to get up and go on
and not to quit after we had erred or fallen.
There is a quality in the people that overcomes
discouragement and challenges defeat.

—ARNOLD CRAFT

I always seem to get inspiration and renewed vitality with this great novel land of yours which sticks up out of the Atlantic.

—WINSTON CHURCHILL

The American, by nature, is forward-looking—an inventor and a builder who is best when called upon to build greatly.

—JOHN F. KENNEDY

It was Ben Franklin who chose the motto on our dollar bill—*Annuit Coeptis*—"Be favorable to bold enterprises." Franklin saw a nation of impossible dreamers whose innovative spirit would help all humanity...if we could only set it free.

—B.J. MARSHALL

The fulfillment of the American promise
was considered inevitable because it was
based upon a combination of self-interest and
the natural goodness of human nature.

—HERBERT CROLY

As a New World, many Americans believe their
country to be the best—best hope of the world, a place
of youth, of new beginnings, of blooming. Even those
who believe that America is, in reality, no such place
of hope or virtue believe it somehow ought to be.

—JAMES O. ROBERTSON

We take nothing for granted; we accept nothing
as perfect; we define nothing as the final end.

—FRANK TANNENBAUM

That's what education means—
to be able to do what you've never done before.

—GEORGE H. PALMER

That's what freedom is all about—
a chance to become better.

—ALBERT CAMUS

More material progress has been made during
the past one hundred and fifty years under the
American system of business than during
all the preceding centuries in world history.
This record of achievement is a challenge
to those who would attack that system.

—KARL T. COMPTON

Every great advance has issued
from a new audacity of imagination.

—JOHN DEWEY

Nothing so challenges the American spirit as
tackling the biggest job on earth. Americans are
stimulated by the big job—the Panama Canal,
Boulder Dam, Grand Coulee, Lower Colorado
River developments, the tallest building in
the world, the mightiest battleship.

—LYNDON B. JOHNSON

One comes to the United States—always,
no matter how often—to see the future.

—EHUD YONAY

Progress results only from the fact that there are some men and women who refuse to believe that what they know to be right cannot be done.

—RUSSELL DAVENPORT

The Wright Brothers flew right through the smokescreen of impossibility.

—CHARLES KETTERING

Success...Four flights thursday morning... All against twenty-one mile winds...Started from level with engine power alone...Average speed through air thirty-one miles...Longest 59 seconds...Inform press...Home Christmas.

—ORVILLE AND WILBUR WRIGHT 12/17/03 (TELEGRAM TO THEIR DAD FROM KITTY HAWK)

Exploration is really the
essence of the human spirit.

—FRANK BORMAN

Always the path of American destiny
has been into the unknown. Always there arose
enough reserves of strength, balances of sanity,
portions of wisdom to carry the nation through
to a fresh start with ever-renewing vitality.

—CARL SANDBURG

Invention triggers invention; ideas build on
ideas. The tea kettle led Fulton to the primitive
steam engine, which led to the gas combustion
engine, which led to the modern rocket propulsion
system—which took us to the moon and back.

—DAN ZADRA

Americans will reach the moon by
standing on each other's shoulders.

—JOHN F. KENNEDY

We landed on the Sea of Tranquility,
in the cool of the early lunar morning.
The plaque on the Eagle which summarized our
hopes bears this message: "Here men from the
planet Earth first set foot upon the moon."

—NEIL A. ARMSTRONG

America is now a space-faring nation,
a frontier good for millions of years. The only
time remotely comparable was when Columbus
discovered a whole new world.

—JAMES MCDONNELL

Science and time and necessity have propelled
the United States to be the general store for the
world, merchants in everything new and possible.
Most of all, merchants for a better way of life.

—LADY BIRD JOHNSON

Nothing is impossible in the United States.

—EVE CURIE

Americans have always assumed, subconsciously,
that all problems can be solved; that every story
has a happy ending; that the application of
enough energy and goodwill can make everything
come out right. In view of our history, this
assumption is probably well-founded.

—ADLAI E. STEVENSON

We are a great heart people.

—PEARL BAILEY

Help wanted. Long hours. No pay. High stress. Lots of travel. Terrible working conditions. Hurry, these positions are filling fast.

—PEACE CORPS AD

Before the Peace Corps, the only Americans the poor Venezuelans ever saw were riding around in Cadillacs. They supposed all Americans to be rich, selfish, callous, reactionary. The Peace Corps has shown them an entirely different kind of American.

—ALLAN STEWART,
U.S. AMBASSADOR TO VENEZUELA

When an American says that he loves
his country, he means not only that he loves the
New England hills, the prairies glistening in the
sun, the great mountains, and the sea. He means
that he loves an inner air, an inner light.

—ADLAI E. STEVENSON

★

The things that the flag stands for were created by
the experiences of a great people. Everything that
it stands for was written by their lives. The flag is
the embodiment, not of sentiment, but of history.

—WOODROW WILSON

★

Sure I wave the American flag.
Do you know a better flag to wave?

—JOHN WAYNE

The Dumbest Person In The World:
How dumb? Very dumb. It's the American who
knocks what he's got. A country of unbounded
beauty. Almost unlimited natural resources.
A judicial system that is the envy of the rest of the
world. Food so plentiful overeating is a problem.
A press nobody can dominate. A ballot box nobody
can stuff. Churches of your choice. One hundred
million jobs. Freedom to go anywhere you want,
with the planes, cars and highways to get you
there. Social Security. Medicare. Unemployment
insurance. Public schools and plentiful scholar-
ships. Opportunity to become a millionaire. Okay,
complainer, what's your second choice? Go.

—GRAY MATTER,
UNITED TECHNOLOGIES CORPORATION

The history of the building of the American nation is a huge laboratory experiment in understanding and in solving the problems that will confront the entire world tomorrow.

—NICHOLAS MURRAY BUTLER

There is nothing wrong with America that cannot be cured by what is right with America.

—PRESIDENT BILL CLINTON

★

The cynics were wrong, the heart of America is strong; it's good and true. We're seeing rededication to bedrock values of faith, family, work, neighborhood, peace, and freedom—values that help bring us together as one people.

—RONALD REAGAN

In this trial (9/11), we have been reminded, and the world has seen, that our fellow Americans are generous and kind, resourceful and brave. We see our national character in rescuers working past exhaustion; in long lines of blood donors; in thousands of citizens who have asked to work and serve in any way possible. In these acts, and in many others, Americans showed a deep commitment to one another, and an abiding love for our country. Today we feel what Franklin Roosevelt called the warm courage of national unity. This is a unity of every faith, and every background.

—PRESIDENT GEORGE W. BUSH,
THREE DAYS AFTER 9/11

LAND WHERE M

Y FATHERS DIED

Put none but

Americans on

guard tonight.

—GEORGE WASHINGTON

Democracy is never a final achievement.
It is a call to untiring effort, to continual
sacrifice and to the willingness, if necessary,
to die in its defense. The cost of freedom is always
high, but Americans have always paid it.

—JOHN F. KENNEDY

America is a nation full of good fortune, with
so much to be grateful for. But we are not spared
from suffering. In every generation, the world has
produced enemies of human freedom. They have
attacked America, because we are freedom's home
and defender. And the commitment of our
fathers is now the calling of our time.

—PRESIDENT GEORGE W. BUSH,
THREE DAYS AFTER 9/11

It is our duty still to endeavor to avoid war;
but if it shall actually take place, no matter by
whom brought on, we must defend ourselves.

—THOMAS JEFFERSON

If one asks me the meaning of our flag, I say
to him: Under this banner rode Washington and
his armies. This banner streamed in light over the
soldiers' heads at Valley Forge and at Morristown.
It crossed the waters roiling with ice at Trenton,
and when its stars gleamed in the morning
with a victory, a new day of hope dawned on
the despondency of this nation.

—HENRY WARD BEECHER

We here highly resolve...that this nation,
under God, shall have a new birth of freedom,
and the government of the people,
by the people, and for the people,
shall not perish from the earth.

—ABRAHAM LINCOLN

Those who would give up essential liberty,
to purchase a little temporary safety,
deserve neither liberty nor safety.

—BENJAMIN FRANKLIN

Being courageous requires no exceptional
qualifications...It is an opportunity that
sooner or later is presented to us all.

—JOHN F. KENNEDY

The condition upon which God hath
given liberty to men is eternal vigilance.

—JOHN P. CURRAN

These are the times that try men's souls.
The summer soldier and the sunshine patriot will,
in this crisis, shrink from the service of their
country; but he that stands it now, deserves the
love and thanks of every man and woman.

—THOMAS PAINE

Freedom is not a heritage, it is a challenge.
And preservation of freedom, whether in the
United States or elsewhere is a fresh
challenge for each generation.

—C. DONALD DALLAS

LAND WHERE MY FATHERS DIED

When you go home, tell them of us and say,
"For their tomorrow, we gave our today."

—THE KOHIMA EPITAPH,
MEDAL OF HONOR MEMORIAL

France was a land, England was a people, but
America, having about it still that quality of the
idea, was harder to utter—it was the graves at
Shiloh, and the tired, drawn, nervous faces of
its great men, and the country boys dying in the
Argonne. It was a willingness of the heart.

—F. SCOTT FITZGERALD

Here rest in glory, an American soldier,
known but to God.

—INSCRIPTION ON THE TOMB OF THE UNKNOWN SOLDIER

The nations of the world have seen our young soldiers in action. They have seen their courage and strength, yes. But off the battlefield they have also seen and admired the human kindness and the tolerance of the men and women who went overseas for us and for them.

—GEORGE SLOAN

America's love has never been equaled in human history. She turns her cheek seventy times seven. She fights only to defend her family. But when she has defeated her enemies she binds their wounds, feeds their children, pays their bills and hands them billions of dollars to restore them to an honorable place among the nations of the world.

—EMMETT MCLOUGHLIN

The eyes of the world are upon you.
The hopes and prayers of liberty-loving
people everywhere march with you.

—GEN. DWIGHT D. EISENHOWER,
TO HIS TROOPS, D-DAY, JUNE 6, 1944

The whole fury and might of the
enemy must very soon be turned on us.
Hitler knows that he will have to break us in the
Island or lose the war. If we can stand up to him,
all Europe may be free and the life of the world
may move forward into broad, sunlit uplands.
But if we fail, then the whole world, including
all that we have known and cared for, will
sink into the abyss of a new Dark Age.

—PRIME MINISTER WINSTON CHURCHILL

Today, the flags of freedom
fly all over Europe.

—HARRY S. TRUMAN,
VE-DAY, MAY 8, 1945

They said we were soft, that we
would not fight, that we could not win.
We are not a warlike nation. We do not
go to war for gain or for territory;
we go to war for principles, and we
produce young men like these.

—HARRY S. TRUMAN

This country will remain the land of the free only
so long as it remains the home of the brave.

—ELMER DAVIS

Millions have visited the Vietnam
Veterans Memorial. Each walks through
a sea of names and wonders, "Who are these
58,220 men and women?" Mothers. Fathers.
Sisters. Brothers. Friends. Loved Ones.
These are Americans who, in the eloquent
words of Abraham Lincoln, "gave their
last full measure of devotion."

—JAN C. SCRUGGS, FOUNDER
VIETNAM VETERANS MEMORIAL FUND

★

I feel an obligation to let the world know how
proud we are of those who served in Vietnam.
Their sacrifice has made a difference to the world
in countless positive ways. One change is that
our government is no longer so willing to get
involved in conflicts without a clear objective.

—J. CRAIG VENTER, PH.D., VIETNAM VETERAN

Let those returned stand straight and tall,
And remember those who gave their all.
Remembering those who fell that day,
And those we left so far away.
Let's now forget the drums of war,
Whose faded sounds we'll ever mourn.
They served in hell, they've earned their rest,
In heaven's arms they've passed God's test.
Two walls of stone, names forever engraved,
A diamond for those who've passed away,
A cross for those whose fate unknown,
A circle for them who may still come home.

—SSGT. FREDERICK E. OWENS, SR.
1ST SPECIAL FORCES, 5TH GROUP, VIETNAM
SALUTE TO THE VIETNAM VET

If a man hasn't discovered something
that he will die for, he isn't fit to live.

—MARTIN LUTHER KING

★

In the long history of the world, only a
few generations have been granted the role
of defending freedom in its hour of maximum
danger. I do not shrink from this responsibility—
I welcome it. I do not believe that any of us would
exchange places with any other people or any
other generation. The energy, faith, the devotion
which we bring to this endeavor will light our
country and all who serve it—and the glow
from that fire can truly light the world.

—JOHN F. KENNEDY

Our forbearance should never be
misunderstood. Our reluctance for conflict
should not be misjudged as failure of will.
When action is required to preserve our national
security and freedom, we will act decisively.

—PRESIDENT RONALD REAGAN

It is to the United States that all freedom-
loving people look for the light and the hope
of the world. Unless we dedicate ourselves
completely to this struggle, unless we combat
hunger with food, fear with trust, suspicion
with faith, fraud with justice—and threats with
power, nations will surrender to the futility
and hopelessness on which wars feed.

—GEN. OMAR N. BRADLEY

LAND WHERE MY FATHERS DIED

We're going to rush the hijackers.

—JEREMY GLICK, UNITED AIRLINES FLIGHT 93
(FINAL WORDS BY CELL PHONE TO HIS WIFE)

We have to accept the risk as
part of the job. Sometimes in this job,
"goodbye" really is "goodbye."

—RAY DOWNEY, NYC FIRE CHIEF
(TWO WEEKS BEFORE LOSING HIS LIFE
AT THE WORLD TRADE CENTER)

What could have destroyed us made us stronger,
thanks to the heroes and volunteers who turned
the worst attack on American soil into the most
successful rescue operation in American history.

—NEW YORK CITY MAYOR RUDY GIULIANI

Great harm has been done to us.
We have suffered great loss. And in our
grief and anger we have found our mission and
our moment. Freedom and fear are at war, and the
great achievement of our time, and the great hope
of every time—now depends on us. Our Nation—
this generation—will lift a dark threat of violence
from our people and our future. We will rally
the world to this cause, by our efforts and by our
courage…We will not tire, we will not falter,
and we will not fail.

—GEORGE W. BUSH,
THREE DAYS AFTER 9/11

Our job is by no means finished, but our nation
has passed the first test well.

—TIME MAGAZINE, 12/31/01

LAND OF THE P

LGRIMS' PRIDE

If I have been able to see
farther than others, it is
because I have stood
on the shoulders of giants.

—SIR ISAAC NEWTON

Remember always that all of us,
and you and I especially, are descended
from immigrants and revolutionists.

—FRANKLIN D. ROOSEVELT

We are descended in blood and in spirit from
revolutionaries and rebels—men and women
who dared to dissent from accepted honest
dissent with disloyal subversion.

—DWIGHT D. EISENHOWER

Our nation was born when 56 patriots got mad
enough to sign the Declaration of Independence.
Getting mad in a constructive way is good for
the soul, and the country, and the world.

—LEE IACOCCA

He is an American, who, leaving behind him all his ancient prejudices and manners, receives new ones from the new mode of life he has embraced. Here individuals of all nations are melted into a new race of men, whose labors and posterity will one day cause great changes in the world.

—MICHEL GUILLAUME SAINT JEAN DE CREVECOEUR, LETTER FROM AN AMERICAN FARMER

The Wilderness masters the colonist. It puts him in a birch canoe. It strips off the garments of civilization and arrays him in the hunting shirt and the moccasin. Little by little he transforms the wilderness, but the outcome is not the old Europe. Here is a new product that is American.

—FREDERICK JACKSON TURNER

From the beginning
America was a place to be discovered.

—PETER SCHRAG

The whole history of our continent
is a history of imagination. Men imagined
land and sea and found it. Men imagined the
forests, the Great Plains, the rivers, the mountains
and found these plains and mountains.
They came, as the great explorers crossed the
Atlantic, because of the imagination of their
minds—because they imagined a better,
a more beautiful, freer, happier world.

—ARCHIBALD MACLEISH

This was the secret of America:
a nation of people with the fresh memory
of old traditions who dared to explore new
frontiers, people eager to build lives for
themselves in a spacious society that did not
restrict their freedom of choice and action.

—JOHN F. KENNEDY

Coming to America has always been hard.
It is foolish to forget where you come from, and
that, in the case of the United States, is almost
always somewhere else. The true authentic
American is a pilgrim with a small "p" armed
with little more than the phrase, "I wish…"

—ANNA QUINDLEN

America lives in the heart of every man
everywhere who wished to find a region where he
is free to work out his destiny as he chooses.

—WOODROW WILSON

★

This country was not built by those who
relied on somebody else to take care of them.
It was built by men and women who relied on
themselves, who dared to shape their own lives,
who had enough courage to blaze new trails with
enough confidence in themselves to take the
necessary risks. This self-reliance is our American
legacy—a precious ingredient in our national
character, one which we must not lose.

—J. OLLIE EDMUNDS

So at last I was going to America!
Really, really going, at last! The boundaries burst.
The arch of heaven soared. A million suns shone
out for every star. The winds rushed in from outer
space, roaring in my ears, "America! America!"

—MARY ANTIN

O beautiful for pilgrim feet,
Whose stern, impassioned stress
A thoroughfare for freedom beat
Across the wilderness!
America! America!
God mend thine every flaw,
Confirm thy soul in self-control,
Thy Liberty in law.

—KATHERINE LEE BATES,
AMERICA THE BEAUTIFUL

Once I thought to write a history of
the immigrants in America. Then I discovered
that the immigrants *were* American history.

—OSCAR HANDLIN

Americans have always been eager
for travel, that being how they got to
the new world in the first place.

—OTTO FRIEDRICH

Give me your tired, your poor,
Your huddled masses yearning to breathe free,
The wretched refuse of your teeming shore.
Send these, the homeless, tempest-tossed, to me,
I lift my lamp beside the golden door!

—EMMA LAZARUS

America has been another name for opportunity.

—FREDERICK JACKSON TURNER

Of all the nations in the world, the
United States was built in nobody's image. It was
the land of the unexpected, of unbounded hope,
of ideals, of quest for an unknown perfection.

—DANIEL J. BOORSTIN

For this is what America is all about.
It is the uncrossed desert and the unclimbed ridge.
It is the star that is not reached and the harvest
that is sleeping in the unplowed ground.

—LYNDON B. JOHNSON

Only in America could a refugee girl
from Europe become Secretary of State.

—MADELEINE ALBRIGHT

Over the years the ancestors of all of us—some
42 million human beings—have migrated to these
shores. The fundamental, long-time American
attitude has been to ask not where a person comes
from but what are his personal qualities.

—LYNDON B. JOHNSON

The aspiring immigrant is not content to
progress alone. He must take his family
with him as he rises.

—MARY ANTIN, THE PROMISED LAND (1912)

When I was a boy it was a dream,
an incredible place where tolerance was
natural and personal freedom unchallenged.
Even when I learned later that America, too,
had massive problems, I could never forget
what an inspiration it had been to the victims
of persecution, to my family, and to me
during cruel and degrading years.

—HENRY KISSINGER

His foreparents came to America in
immigrant ships. My foreparents came
to America in slave ships. But whatever
the original ships, we are both in
the same boat today.

—JESSE JACKSON

Action is always feasible under the form of government which we have inherited from our ancestors. Our Constitution is so simple and practical that it is possible always to meet extraordinary needs. That is why our constitutional system has proved itself the most superbly enduring political mechanism the modern world has produced. It has met every stress of vast expansion of territory, of foreign wars, of bitter internal strife, or world relations.

—FRANKLIN D. ROOSEVELT

Yes, we did produce a near perfect Republic. But will they keep it? Or, will they, in the enjoyment of plenty, lose the memory of freedom?

—THOMAS JEFFERSON

There is a need for heroism in American life today.

—AGNES MEYER

I pray we are still a young and courageous nation, that we have not grown so old and so soft and so prosperous that all we can think about is to sit back with our arms around our money bags.

—LYNDON B. JOHNSON

Let us once again awaken our American revolution, our pioneer spirit, until it guides the struggles of people everywhere—not with an imperialism of force and fear but with courage and freedom and hope for the future of man.

—JOHN F. KENNEDY

FROM EVERY M

OUNTAINSIDE

Depend upon it

that the lovers

of freedom

will become free.

—EDMUND BURKE

The cause of America is, in great measure,
the cause of all mankind. He that would make
his own liberty secure must guard even
his own enemy from oppression.

—THOMAS PAINE, 1776

Our American friends have done a
marvelous job of reminding us that the high
purpose of freedom is to create it for others.

—PRIME MINISTER TONY BLAIR,
THE UNITED KINGDOM

Everyone wants a voice in human freedom—
the freedom to express our individuality in work
and in life. That's a fire burning inside all of us.

—LECH WALESA, POLAND

The chance to go to school, to earn
a good living, to raise a family. The freedom
to pursue one's hopes and dreams. These are
not just Western ideals, they are the world's.

—INDIRA GANDHI, INDIA

The most powerful and persistent force in the
world today is neither Communism nor capitalism,
neither the bomb nor the missile—it is man's
eternal desire to be free and independent.

—JOHN F. KENNEDY

The West will not contain Communism,
it will transcend Communism.

—PRESIDENT RONALD REAGAN

Governments everywhere arise
either out of the people or over the people.

—THOMAS PAINE

Dictators ride to and fro upon
tigers which they dare not dismount.
And the tigers are getting hungry.

—SIR WINSTON S. CHURCHILL

Throughout the history of mankind there
have been murderers and tyrants; and while
it may seem momentarily that they have the
upper hand, they have always fallen. Always.

—MOHANDAS K. GANDHI

When you stop a dictator there are always risks. But there are greater risks in not stopping a dictator.

—PRIME MINISTER MARGARET THATCHER

Little by little, the nations whose people believe in freedom are becoming united. Good neighbors, when menaced by gangsters, meet and agree on laws for protecting themselves. To lead the way in this direction is America's greatest challenge.

—ESTES KEFAUVER

This is not a battle between the U.S. and terrorism. It's a battle between a free and democratic world against terrorism.

—PRIME MINISTER TONY BLAIR

FROM EVERY MOUNTAINSIDE

You people of the United States have
the wonderfully farseeing conception of being
Democracy's material and spiritual arsenal, to save
the world's highest values from annihilation.

—QUEEN JULIANA,
THE NETHERLANDS

Let us never confuse power with greatness.
Power is not an end in itself, but is an
instrument that must be used toward an end.

—JEANE KIRKPATRICK

★

There are two ways of exerting one's strength—
one is pushing down, the other is pulling up.

—BOOKER T. WASHINGTON

America is great because she is good,
and if America ever ceases to be good,
America will cease to be great.

—ALEXIS DE TOCQUEVILLE

The best way to enhance freedom in
other lands is to demonstrate here that our
democratic system is worthy of emulation.

—JIMMY CARTER

We shall be a city upon the hill,
the eyes of the world are upon us.

—WALLACE DUNNE

It seems to me very important to the idea of
democracy—to the country and to the world
eventually—that all men and women, regardless
of nationality, stand equal under the sky.

—GEORGIA O'KEEFE

We look forward to a world founded upon four
essential human freedoms. The first is freedom of
speech and expression everywhere in the world.
The second is freedom of every person to worship
God in his own way everywhere in the world.
The third is freedom from want, everywhere in
the world. The fourth is freedom from fear…
everywhere in the world.

—FRANKLIN D. ROOSEVELT

God and the politicians willing, the United States
can declare peace upon the world, and win it.

—ELY CULBERTSON

Science has made the dream of
today's reality for all the earth if we have
the courage to build it. American Democracy
must furnish the engineers of world plenty—
the builders of world peace and freedom.

—MARIAN LA SUEUR

The ultimate end of all social change
is to establish the sanctity of human life,
the dignity of man, the right of every
human being to liberty and well-being.

—EMMA GOLDMAN

Brute force, no matter how strongly applied, can never subdue the basic human desire for freedom.

—DALAI LAMA

The word will continue to fly
All over the world
No power can stop it
From landing at any airport
For the word is a bird
That needs no entry visa
For freedom
For democracy

—NABIL JANABI,
IRAQI POET

Mr. Gorbachev, tear down this wall.

—RONALD REAGAN, 1987, AT THE BERLIN WALL

Liberty, once started, is inexorably forward-
thinking, forward-moving, forward-acting.

—ARTHUR TELLER

In this revolution no plans
have been written for retreat.

—MARTIN LUTHER KING, JR.

I have walked the long road to freedom.
I have discovered that after climbing a great hill,
one only finds that there are many more hills
to climb. I have taken a moment here to rest.
But I can only rest a moment, for with freedom
comes responsibilities, and I dare not linger,
for my long walk is not ended.

—NELSON MANDELA, SOUTH AFRICA

Freedom is the first condition of growth.
What you do not make free cannot grow.

—VIVEKANANDA,
INDIAN RELIGIOUS LEADER

True individual freedom cannot exist
without economic security and independence.
People who are hungry and out of a job are the
stuff of which dictatorships are made.

—THEODORE ROOSEVELT

We have a solution for war.
It is to expand the sphere of liberty.

—RUDOLPH RUMMEL

Liberty, when it does begin to take root, is a plant
of rapid growth.

—GEORGE WASHINGTON

All the world wondered as they witnessed
how quickly our people lifted themselves from
humiliation and oppression to the greatest pride.

—CORAZON AQUINO,
PHILIPPINE LEADER

When Americans put their heads on their pillows
at night, I wonder if they realize what a beacon of
hope they are for oppressed people everywhere.

—JANE RICHARDS

LET FREE

OOM RING

We have it in our power

to begin the world again.

—THOMAS PAINE, 1776

I like the dreams of the
future better than the history of the past.

—THOMAS JEFFERSON

There is a New America every morning when we
wake up. It is upon us whether we will it or not.

—ADLAI E. STEVENSON

We're entering our third century now, but
it's wrong to judge our nation by its years.
The calendar can't measure America because
we were meant to be an endless experiment
in freedom, with no limit to our reaches,
no boundaries to what we can do,
no end point to our hopes.

—PRESIDENT RONALD REAGAN

I hope the day will never come when
the American nation will be the champion of
the status quo. Once that happens, we shall have
forfeited the support of those who believe that they
can make a better world and of those who dream
dreams and want those dreams to come true.

—JOHN FOSTER DULLES

Now the trumpet summons us again—
not as a call to bear arms, though arms we need—
not as a call to battle, though embattled we are—
but a call to bear the burden of the long twilight
struggle, year in and year out, rejoicing in hope,
patient in tribulation—a struggle against
the common enemies of man: tyranny,
poverty, disease and war itself.

—PRESIDENT JOHN F. KENNEDY

Choose to live,
work and succeed in the most
powerful nation on earth: Imagination.

—DAN ZADRA

America is too great for small dreams.

—PRESIDENT RONALD REAGAN

There are no limits on our future
if we don't put limits on our people.

—JACK KEMP

If we're strong enough,
there are no precedents.

—F. SCOTT FITZGERALD

All limitations are self-imposed.

—HEIDI WILLS

No one is going to diminish the spirit
of this country.

—PRESIDENT GEORGE W. BUSH

We have enough people
who tell it like it is—now we could
use a few who tell it like it can be.

—ROBERT ORBEN

This I know. This I believe with all my heart.
If we want a free and peaceful world, if we want
to make deserts bloom and man to grow to greater
dignity as a human being—we can do it!

—ELEANOR ROOSEVELT

If we want to make something really superb of our
community, our country and this planet, there is
nothing whatsoever that can stop us.

—SHEPHERD MEAD

The best hope of solving all our
problems lies in harnessing the diversity,
the energy and the creativity of all our people.

—ROGER WILKINS

Together, we have the power, knowledge
and equipment to build a world beyond our
wonder. Only loss of nerve can defeat us.
That is all—loss of nerve.

—JAMES DILLET FREEMAN

Determine that the thing shall be done,
and then we shall find the way.

—ABRAHAM LINCOLN

Do not wait for leaders;
do it alone, person to person.

—MOTHER TERESA

But where was I to start? The world is so vast.
I shall start with the country I know best, my own.
But my country is so very large. I had better start
with my town. But my town, too, is large. I had
better start with my street. No, my home. No, my
family. Never mind. I shall start with myself.

—ELIE WIESEL

The truth of the matter is that you always know
the right thing to do. The hard part is doing it.

—GEN. NORMAN SCHWARZKOPF

Destiny is not a matter of chance,
it is a matter of choice; it is not a thing
to be waited for, it is a thing to be achieved.

—WILLIAM JENNINGS BRYAN

Let every man or woman here, remember this,
that if you wish to be great at all, you must
begin where you are and what you are, in your
town, now. He that can give to his city any energy
or spirit, he who can be a good citizen while he
lives here, he that can make better homes, he that
can be a blessing whether he works in the shop or
sits behind the counter or keeps house, whatever
be his life, he who would be great anywhere
must first be great in his own town.

—RUSSELL H. CONWELL

How, then, shall we live?
How must we live to preserve free societies
and to be worthy of the blood and the pain?
This is the unfinished business of our century.

—THEOLOGIAN MICHAEL NOVAK

★

In every community there is work to be done.
In every nation, there are wounds to heal.
In every heart there is the power to do it.

—MARIANNE WILLIAMSON

★

Let us live our lives so that our children
can tell their children that we not only stood for
something wonderful—we acted on it.

—DAN ZADRA

Each one of us will one day be judged
by our standard of life, not by our standard
of living; by our measure of giving...not by our
measure of wealth...by our simple goodness...
not by our seeming greatness.

—WILLIAM WARD

I look forward to an America
which will not be afraid of grace and
beauty, which will protect the beauty of our
natural environment, which will preserve
the great old American houses and squares and
parks of our national past and which will build
handsome and balanced cities for our future.

—PRESIDENT JOHN F. KENNEDY

People who develop the habit of thinking
of themselves as world citizens are fulfilling
the first requirement of sanity in our time.

—NORMAN COUSINS

What was most significant about the
lunar voyage was not that men set foot on
the moon but that they set eye on the earth.

—NORMAN COUSINS

To see the earth as we now see it,
small and beautiful in that eternal silence
where it floats, is to see ourselves as riders
on the earth together, brothers on that bright
loveliness in the unending night.

—ARCHIBALD MACLEISH,
THE NEW YORK TIMES, 12/25/68

The first day or so we all pointed to
our countries. Then the third or fourth day
we were pointing to our continents. By the
fifth day we were aware of only one earth.

—SULTAN BINSULMAN AL-SAUD,
SAUDI ARABIAN ASTRONAUT

We have to find ways of organizing
ourselves with the rest of humanity.
It has to be everybody or nobody.

—R. BUCKMINSTER FULLER

There is no such thing as "them" and "us."
In a world this size, there can only be "we"—
all of us working together.

—JOHN HOLMES

Science has made the world
a neighborhood, but it will take love
to make it a sisterhood, a brotherhood,
a community of peace with justice.

—ELIZABETH M. SCOTT

★

All this will not be finished in the first one
hundred days. Nor will it be finished in the
first one thousand days, nor in the life of this
administration, nor even perhaps in our lifetime.
But let us begin. In your hands, my fellow
citizens, more than mine, will rest the
final success or failure of our course.

—JOHN F. KENNEDY

We travel together, passengers
on a little space ship, dependant on
its vulnerable reserves of air and soil;
all committed for our safety, to its security
and peace; preserved from annihilation only
by the care, the work, and I will say, the love
we give our fragile craft. We cannot maintain
it half fortunate, half miserable, half confident,
half despairing, half slave—to the ancient
enemies of man—half free in a liberation
of resources undreamed of until this day.
No craft, no crew can travel safely with such
vast contradictions. On their resolution
depends the survival of us all.

—ADLAI E. STEVENSON

The Bill of Rights
Ten Pillars of Freedom

To ensure that the individual rights of every citizen would be spelled out and protected, the First Congress of the United States proposed a list of amendments to the Constitution. The following is a transcription of the first 10 amendments to the U.S. Constitution in their original form. These amendments were ratified December 15, 1791, and form what is now known and admired throughout the world as the "Bill of Rights."

Amendment I

Congress shall make no law respecting an establishment of religion, or prohibiting the free exercise thereof; or abridging the freedom of speech, or of the press; or the right of the people peaceably to assemble, and to petition the Government for a redress of grievances.

Amendment II

A well regulated Militia, being necessary to the security of a free State, the right of the people to keep and bear Arms, shall not be infringed.

Amendment III

No Soldier shall, in time of peace be quartered in any house, without the consent of the Owner, nor in time of war, but in a manner to be prescribed by law.

Amendment IV

The right of the people to be secure in their persons, houses, papers, and effects, against unreasonable searches and seizures, shall not be violated, and no Warrants shall issue, but upon probable cause, supported by Oath or affirmation, and particularly describing the place to be searched, and the persons or things to be seized.

Amendment V

No person shall be held to answer for a capital, or otherwise infamous crime, unless on a presentment or indictment of a Grand Jury, except in cases arising in the land or naval forces, or in the Militia, when in actual service in time of War or public danger;

★

nor shall any person be subject for the same offence to be twice put in jeopardy of life or limb; nor shall be compelled in any criminal case to be a witness against himself, nor be deprived of life, liberty, or property, without due process of law; nor shall private property be taken for public use, without just compensation.

Amendment VI

In all criminal prosecutions, the accused shall enjoy the right to a speedy and public trial, by an impartial jury of the State and district wherein the crime shall have been committed, which district shall have been previously ascertained by law, and to be informed of the nature and cause of the accusation; to be confronted with the witnesses against him; to have compulsory process for obtaining witnesses in his favor, and to have the Assistance of Counsel for his defense.

Amendment VII

In suits at common law, where the value in controversy shall exceed twenty dollars, the right of trial by jury shall be preserved, and no fact tried by a jury, shall be otherwise reexamined in any Court of the United States, than according to the rules of the common law.

Amendment VIII

Excessive bail shall not be required, nor excessive fines imposed, nor cruel and unusual punishments inflicted.

Amendment IX

The enumeration in the Constitution, of certain rights, shall not be construed to deny or disparage others retained by the people.

Amendment X

The powers not delegated to the United States by the Constitution, nor prohibited by it to the States, are reserved to the States respectively, or to the people.

*The New Frontier
of which I speak is not
a set of promises, it is a set
of challenges. It sums up
not what is offered to you
but what is asked of you.*

—JOHN F. KENNEDY